colored pencil on copper jewelry

ROXAN O'BRIEN

colored
pencil
on copper
jewelry

ROXAN
O'BRIEN

STACKPOLE
BOOKS

Guilford, Connecticut

Published by Stackpole Books
An imprint of Globe Pequot

Distributed by NATIONAL BOOK NETWORK
800-462-6420

British Library Cataloguing in Publication Information available
Library of Congress Cataloging-in-Publication Data available

ISBN 978-0-8117-1711-3 (paperback)
ISBN 978-0-8117-6585-5 (e-book)

∞™ The paper used in this publication meets the minimum requirements of American National Standard for Information Sciences—Permanence of Paper for Printed Library Materials, ANSI/NISO Z39.48-1992.

First Edition

Printed in the United States of America

CONTENTS

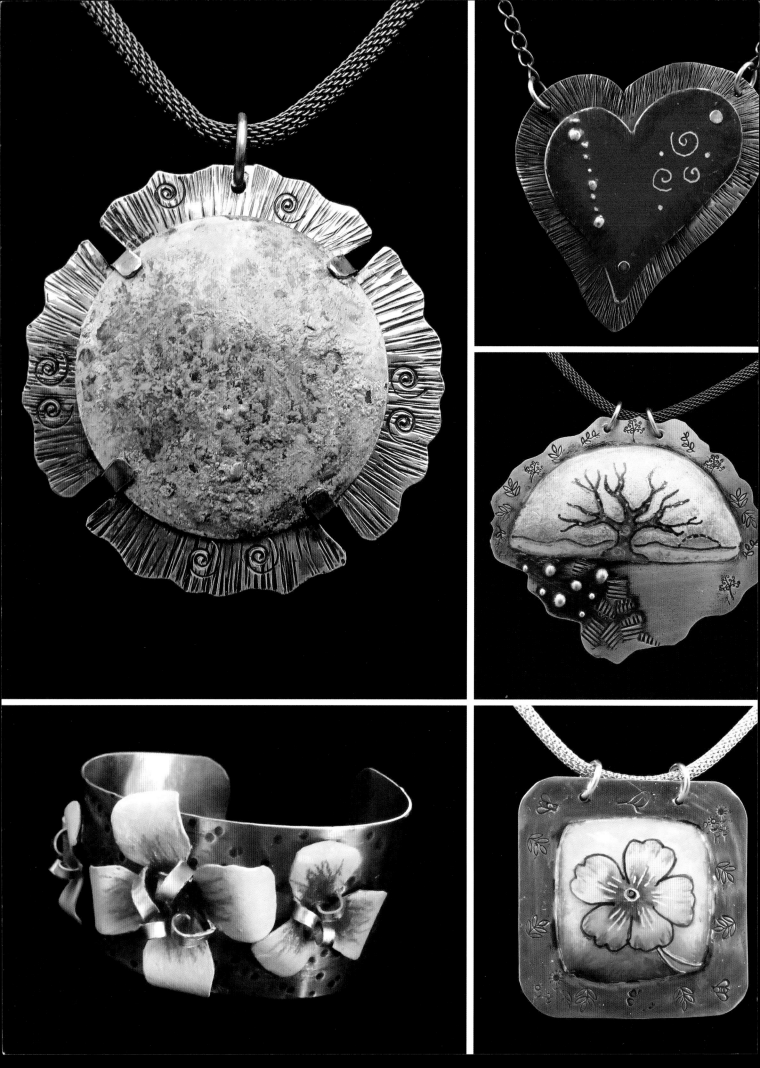

INTRODUCTION

After many years working with a broad range of techniques as a silversmith and in glass beads, I wanted to add more color and texture to my work. I explored working with enamels, doing cloisonné and other enameling processes, but while beautiful it takes many hours of labor, and it still didn't allow me the freedom to use my skills as an artist at the level I desired. When the price of silver skyrocketed, I started to look for alternative metals that weren't being used very much and were more affordable—which is when I found the benefits of working in copper.

Then I discovered a little-known technique, using colored pencils on metal. After several years of experimenting and refining the technique, I devised an easy way to get what I was looking for. What I like about this technique is that it gives the look of an enameled piece without the use of a kiln, and therefore is more accessible to the novice jewelry maker and advanced artist alike.

This book is designed to appeal to all levels of jewelry making, but in no way is it limited to the novice. My hope for this book is to give the reader an in-depth understanding on how to use the colored pencil technique as well as other simple and easy metal coloring techniques with minimal amounts of tools and time to create beautiful jewelry. Where possible I have adapted alternative tools you can easily find around the house or at your local hardware or craft store.

I recommend you wear safety glasses when working with metal and abide by standard safety precautions when working with all tools. For the projects in this book we will be working with copper since it is relatively inexpensive and easily available from most suppliers.

Inspiration

My journey to discovering colored pencil technique led me to research the works of Marilyn da Silva and Helen Shirk, both renowned metalsmiths who use a similar coloring technique on metal sculptures. The richness of color they get is breathtaking. I suggest that you take a look at their beautiful work for ideas in the use of texture and color.

After years of experimenting, I came up with my own, simpler way to create with colored pencils on metal that is permanent, with vivid color and detail of design. My work is created in the footsteps of all those who came before me, and I am grateful that I can carry on and add my twist to this process.

I hope this book will inspire you to take what you learn here and transform it into your own voice. I encourage you to explore your creativity. On the following pages are a few samples of my work using the techniques outlined in this book.

Green leaf on copper pendant.
The center of this piece was created using a round silhouette die and the colored pencil technique with a Zentangle design in blues and green, highlighted using a micro engraver. The exposed copper was textured with leaf design metal stamps and dimple pliers with black patina and sealed with ProtectaClear.

Green leaf on nickel silver pendant.
The center was created with a round silhouette die and the colored pencil technique with a Zentangle design in blues, grays, and greens, highlighted using a micro engraver. The exposed nickel silver was decorated with leaf metal stamps, dimple pliers, and black patina. It was sealed with ProtectaClear.

Chickadee on copper pendant.
This bird was created with a silhouette die and the colored pencil technique in grays, black, white, and taupe. The exposed copper was textured with a bird and leaf design metal stamp and black patina. It was sealed with ProtectaClear, and patina brass bird feet were added.

Oval geometric on copper pendant.
This piece was created with an oval silhouette die and the colored pencil technique in black, green, blue, orange, gray, and purple. The exposed copper was designed with a texturing hammer, spiral metal stamp, and black patina, etched with a micro engraver and sealed with ProtectaClear.

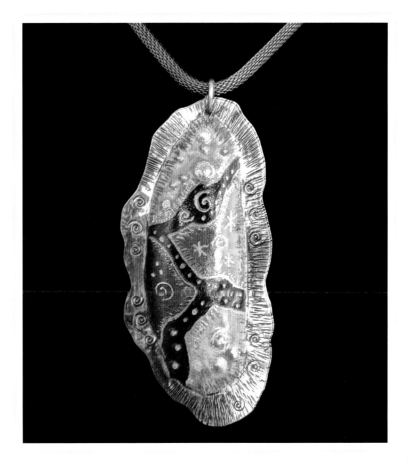

Waves of color necklace.
The pieces that make up this necklace were made with silhouette dies on copper and the colored pencil technique in black, lime green, purple, blue, and turquoise. The exposed copper was designed with a texturing hammer, dimple pliers, and black patina, etched with a micro engraver and sealed with ProtectaClear.

Birds of a feather necklace.
The bird is made with a silhouette die on copper and the colored pencil technique in green, yellow, and beige, sealed with ProtectaClear. The bird is surrounded by glass seed beads, topaz Swarovski crystal, and larger glass beads.

Tree of life copper pendant.
This pendant was created with a silhouette die and the colored pencil technique with blue sky, orange sun, and brown tree. The stars and spirals were highlighted with a micro engraver. The exposed copper was textured with a hammer, dimple pliers, and black patina. The branch was cut out with a jewelry saw and sealed with ProtectaClear.

Blooming flowers bracelets.
Here are three versions of the Blooming Flowers Bracelet project demonstrated in this book (see page 53). The bracelets are decorated with colored pencil on copper and sealed with ProtectaClear.

Blue jay pendant.
This bird was created with a silhouette die and the colored pencil technique in grays, black, white, and blues. The exposed copper was textured with a bird and leaf design metal stamp and black patina. It was sealed with ProtectaClear, and patina brass bird feet were added.

Paradise garden.
The bird was created with a silhouette die and colored pencils on copper and applied to the center of the piece. The bird is surrounded by glass seed beads, Swarovski crystals, and glass beads and finished with fringe in crystals and glass dangles.

Tools and Supplies

In this chapter, I introduce you to the basic tools you will need when working with copper and colored pencils. When you first start out, buy the tools you can afford and adapt things you may already own. You don't have to buy expensive, high-end tools. Until you learn how to use your tools properly, go to garage sales or flea markets to get hammers and other tools. After some time experiencing different techniques you may want to upgrade, but to start out buying very expensive tools in the beginning is unwise. Learn to adapt tools for your use, like bolts, nails, and kitchen tools.

Tools

- [ ] Hammers (for chasing and texturing)
- [ ] Tweezers
- [ ] Fire brick
- [ ] Small micro torch
- [ ] Heat gun or hair dryer
- [ ] Metal shears
- [ ] Jewelry saw and blades
- [ ] Anvil or stamping block
- [ ] Glass or plastic container with lid
- [ ] Pliers: round and flat
- [ ] Forming pliers
- [ ] Hole punches: 1.25 mm, 1.5 mm, 1.8 mm, and larger
- [ ] Pen or micro engraver, or metal scribe
- [ ] Wire cutters: flush
- [ ] Small jewelry files
- [ ] Rolling pin or bracelet mandrel
- [ ] Safety glasses
- [ ] Metal stamps
- [ ] Dimple pliers: 2 mm or 3 mm
- [ ] Dapping block: wooden or metal
- [ ] Tube cutter
- [ ] Hydraulic press
- [ ] Plastic or rawhide hammer

Heat guns are used to speed drying time; they usually come in 15 watts and look like hair dryers but get much hotter and don't blow the air. You can also use a **hair dryer** set on low when a heat gun is called for. You will need a **fire brick** or other heat-resistant surface, **heat-safe tweezers** for picking up hot metal, a **small butane torch** for heat patina, and **safety glasses**. I can't stress this enough: Wear safety glasses when working with metal, especially when cutting rivets.

You will need several **hammers**. A few good ones that will come in handy include riveting (small and large), chasing, plastic, goldsmith, and texturing.

Metal and wood dapping blocks are a good investment to shape metal. A **steel block** or **anvil** is needed when stamping with metal stamps, texturing, and riveting. A **metal bracelet mandrel** comes in handy when making bracelets, but you can also use a rolling pin.

Jewelry saws come in many brands and sizes; I happen to like my German 5-inch saw, which is inexpensive and works well. While a **jeweler's bench** is wonderful to have, you can buy a **portable bench pin** that attaches to a table, which will work just fine.

A **drill press** is another handy tool to have, but make sure you use burr wax on all your drill bits to extend their life, and put a piece of wood under the bit.

You will need a variety of **pliers**: Flat, round, bail-bending pliers, angled, and long flat will come in handy when working with metal. At top is a **center punch** for marking where you will need to drill.

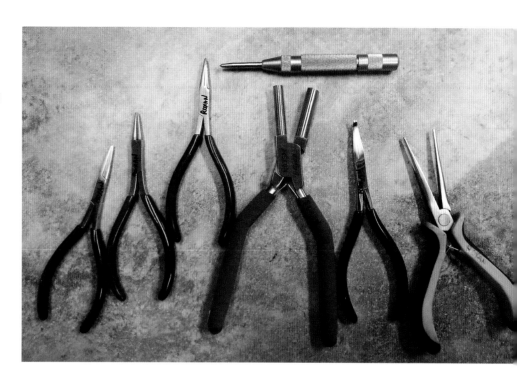

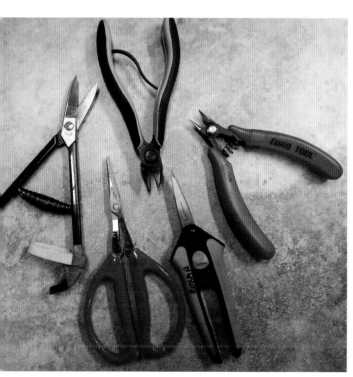

A good pair of **shears** for cutting metal is a good investment. Curved shears help to cut on a curve. I like Joyce Chin shears, but the Fiskars garden shear works and is available at any garden shop. You will also need a pair of **flush cutters** to cut rivets and to cut burrs off your metal.

Hole punches come in several sizes for cutting holes: from left to right are 1.25 mm, 1.5 mm, 1.5 mm long neck, and 1.8 mm. These make it easier to make a hole without buying a drill press.

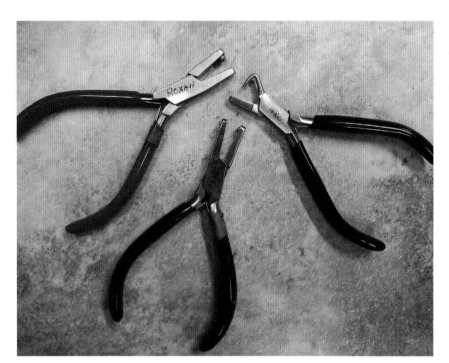

Dimple pliers are one of my go-to texturing tools. They come in several sizes—5 mm, 3 mm, and 1 mm. I mostly use the two smaller ones for jewelry.

I love my battery-operated **micro engraver**, used to highlight areas on my work, but you can use an electric one or a scribe.

Good **jewelry files** are a must. I like the small diamond files, plus: a good flat one, a round one, and an angled one.

A **bezel pusher** is used to set prongs. Left to right: flat bezel pusher, curved bezel pusher, rocker pusher, and small bezel pusher.

A **tube cutter** is a very helpful tool to cut metal tubes, since it is difficult to cut straight without using one.

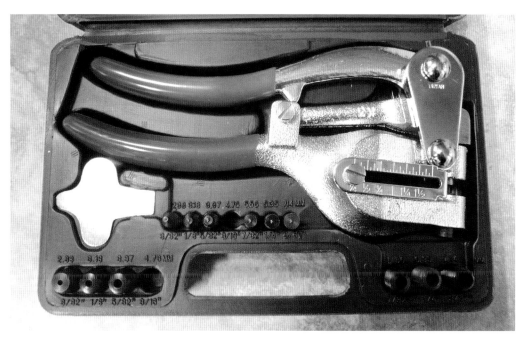

A **large hole punch** comes in handy to cut larger holes. This one is from Euro Tool; it's fairly easy to change the punches, which run from ³⁄₃₂ inch (2.38 mm) to ⁹⁄₃₂ inch (7.14 mm).

Supplies

- [ ] 22- to 24-gauge dead soft copper sheet
- [ ] 2.35 mm copper or brass tubing
- [ ] Jump rings, 16-gauge 9 mm OD (outer diameter)
- [ ] Jewelry saw and saw blades, size 2/0 to 5/0
- [ ] Baking tin (for placing hot metal on after heating)
- [ ] Patina: Jax or Novacan, in black, green, or brown; or liver of sulfur gel
- [ ] Cleaner: Bar Keepers Friend or Bon Ami

- [ ] Denatured alcohol
- [ ] Q-tips
- [ ] ProtectaClear from Everbrite
- [ ] Gesso: gray, white, black, or burnt umber
- [ ] Acrylic spray
- [ ] PrismaColor Premier colored pencils (in the tins only)
- [ ] Turpentine or Turpenoid Natural
- [ ] 18 x ½-inch brass finishing nails or .05-inch or 1.27 mm copper rivets
- [ ] Small plastic containers

- [ ] Paintbrushes: #0 or #1 flat (for use with turpentine to push and blend the colors into the gesso) and #6 or #8 flat (for applying gesso)
- [ ] Sandpaper: medium 250 and fine 650 black wet-dry
- [ ] Sanding blocks in several grades
- [ ] Blue painter's tape
- [ ] Baroque Art Gilders Paste (gold)
- [ ] Pencils and extra-fine felt tip black permanent marker (Sharpie)

Gesso is a water-based mixture of chalk, gypsum, and pigment. It is readily available in many colors, but for most of my work I use gray since it is a neutral color, which allows me to use dark or light pencils. I don't like using the gesso right out of the jar or bottle it comes in, so I put mine in small squeeze bottles for easier use. Gesso is messy, and if it gets on your clothes it will not come out once it dries, so I suggest you wear old clothes or an apron and clean your brush with water as soon as possible after applying the gesso.

You will need both **medium and fine sandpaper**. I use the wet-dry black paper, which I cut into 1-inch squares for easy handling. I also like to use the **small sponge sanding blocks** that are available from beauty supply houses. They are made for use on fingernails, but work wonders on metal, too, and come in coarse, medium, and fine grades. I cut these into thirds for getting into small spaces, especially where it is hard to use a metal jewelry file. Having both small jewelry files along with some larger ones will come in handy when working with metal.

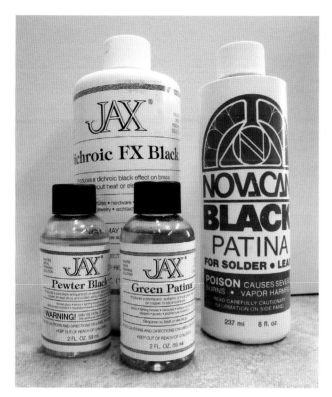

Patina is just a fancy name for tarnish, oxidation, and the natural aging process on metal. We can hasten it by using commercial chemicals such as Jax Green Patina or Novacan Black Patina, or by using things you have around the house and easily available.

Rubber gloves, old toothbrushes, Bar Keepers Friend, Bon Ami, a green Scotch-Brite pad, alcohol, and Q-tips come in handy for cleaning metal before using patina and metal stamps. An old toothbrush works well to scrub your metal with a cleaner to remove any oil. I like the Bon Ami powder or Bar Keepers Friend; both will remove the oil from the metal and are safe for the environment.

A few more supplies to keep on hand include 16-gauge wire to make 9 mm copper jump rings, 1- and 2-inch-diameter 22- to 24-gauge round copper disks, 18 x ½-inch brass nails, ¼-inch x 3.5 mm copper rivets, and a Sharpie pen.

This technique can be used on any metal, but for all the projects in this book we will be using 22- to 24-gauge copper. I get my copper from a roofing company sold as flashing, which comes by the square foot. Unless you have a large bench shear or cutter, don't buy more than a foot at a time, or buy it already cut from a metal jewelry supplier. The roofing copper is between 22 and 24 gauge, which works well for jewelry.

You will need to use **PrismaColor Premier colored pencils**—which come in sets in tins—*no other pencils will work*. These colored pencils contain a higher wax content than other pencils, which is needed for the color to adhere to the prepared metal. While PrismaColor sells many different kinds of colored pencils, make sure that you are getting the Premier colors—not watercolor, Verithin, Scholar, or any other kinds of pencils.

Turpentine is distilled from the resin of a pine tree and is primarily used as a solvent. It must be used in a well-ventilated area. If you are sensitive or have any lung problems, you will want to use a turpentine substitute. There is a brand called **Turpenoid Natural**, which is safe to use and you can buy it odorless. A **small bottle with an eyedropper** is needed to portion out the turpentine, which you will use in minuscule amounts. I like the small condiment cups often used at restaurants for holding gesso and turpentine.

Right: This twelve-pack is the smallest set of PrismaColor Premier colored pencils and the one I recommend you buy to start the projects in this book. Individual pencils are also available in most art and craft stores, but when you buy the pencils in the tin they come already sharpened. When it is time to sharpen your pencil, only use a small handheld pencil sharpener, not a big hand-cranked or electric one. The pencils can break very easily, and you need to take care to sharpen them slowly to avoid this.

ProtectaClear is a product from Everbrite that keeps metal from tarnishing. It comes in both spray and liquid form. This is the best product I have found to keep copper from tarnishing, and it doesn't come off.

    Acrylic spray comes in several finishes, including gloss, satin, and matte. They all work well, so choosing which to use is personal preference; I like the matte finish for a lot of my work. Brand is not as important for your choice of coating. Krylon works well, but so do many other brands.

Baroque Art Gilders Paste and **Viva Inka-Gold** are coloring pastes similar to the consistency of shoe polish that add great highlights to metalwork.

You will need a **glass bowl with lid** for liquid patinas and **small and large plastic containers** for gesso, turpentine, and other uses.

Shaping Metal

While the colored pencil coloring process can be done on flat metal, it is more interesting if done on domed or shaped metal. The best way to shape metal is with a hydraulic press. All the pieces in this book were created on a Harbor Freight 12-ton hydraulic press, but we will also explore less expensive ways to shape metal. You can do many of the same things by using a vise, silicone pot holders, and a silhouette die. I always look for things I can use from hardware stores or flea markets, such as large bolts and shapes that I can press my metal into. I have often used a rolling pin as a mandrel to shape a bracelet. You can also form metal with a dapping block by forcing the metal into the block. You don't always need expensive equipment to shape metal; use what you already have.

Dap and Dapping Blocks

Supplies

- ☐ Round wooden dap
- ☐ Swage dap
- ☐ Dapping block
- ☐ Nylon, plastic, or wood mallet
- ☐ Sandbag
- ☐ Shears or jewelry saw
- ☐ Jewelry files
- ☐ Sandpaper

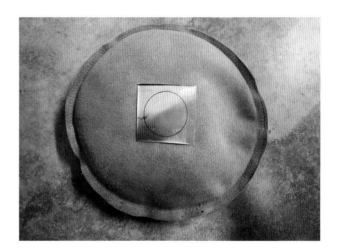

Once you have cut your piece of copper to the size you want, you can shape it by using a dapping tool. I like a wooden swage for oblong or square pieces and a round dapping block for round pieces, both available from a jewelry supply house. When using a wooden dap, make sure you only use a wooden, nylon, or plastic mallet.

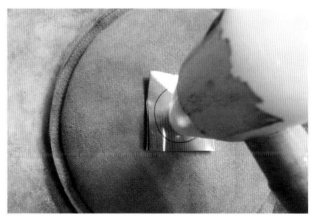

Make a circle, and then shape the piece of copper with a plastic mallet and a sandbag. Once you have given it a little shape, you can move on to a steel dapping block.

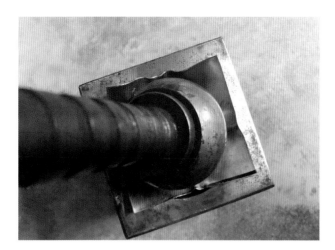

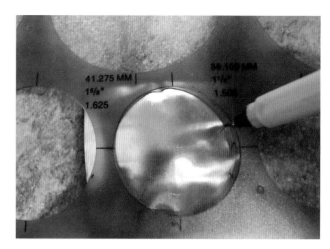

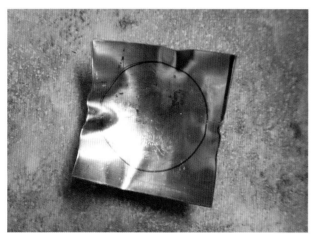

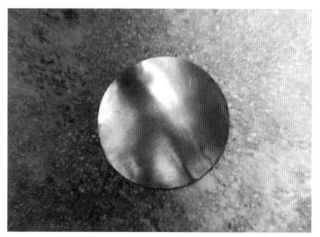

Place the piece in the steel dapping block and continue to deform the copper with a hammer. Don't worry that the shape isn't smooth yet.

Turn the piece over. Using a circle template, draw a circle then cut along the line with a pair of shears or a jewelry saw. File, sand, and smooth any unevenness.

Vise and Dies

Supplies

- [ ] Vise
- [ ] Silicone pot holder
- [ ] Silhouette die
- [ ] Piece of dead soft metal
- [ ] Painter's tape

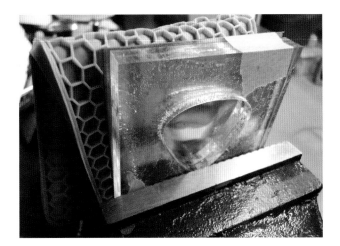

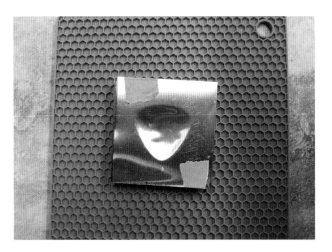

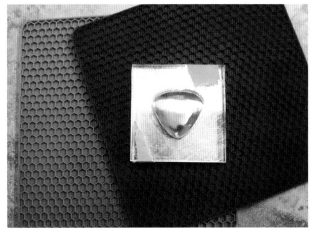

This is the piece I did in the vise. It takes more effort, but it can be done without the use of a hydraulic press.

All you need is a silicone pot holder, a silhouette die, and a piece of dead soft metal. It is always good to use painter's tape to tape the metal to the die. Double up at least one pot holder and put it on one side of the die. Insert it in the vise as far down as you can and squeeze it as tight as you can. You may have to turn the die in the vise to get the metal to deform into the die.

Hydraulic Press and Dies

If you want to invest in a commercial press that is made just for jewelry, there are several available, but they are expensive. The two that I am familiar with are the Bonny Doon and Potter USA, which are both excellent (see Resources on page 87 for suppliers). However, you can get a Harbor Freight press for a lot less, and it works well with silhouette dies or pancake dies. I have a Harbor Freight 12-ton hydraulic press that I use to make all my jewelry. I wouldn't use anything less than the 12-ton press for making pieces with dies.

To use a hydraulic press, you need to either buy dies or make your own. Potter USA and Bonny Doon both make commercial silhouette dies and pancake dies. I make most of my own silhouette dies, but pancake dies are far more difficult to make on your own. I suggest that if you want to use pancake dies you buy them from Potter USA. By making your own dies, you can customize them to your projects. See the next section for my easy and inexpensive die-making process.

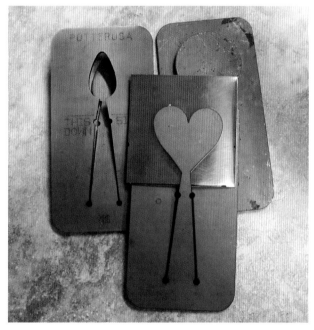

A pancake die is a steel die that will cut a flat shape quickly rather than having to use a jewelry saw. I used the heart pancake die in the heart project in this book. You can use a pancake die in a vise to cut out the piece.

A silhouette die is a die made from steel or acrylic that makes an impression in the metal creating an embossed shape.

Harbor Freight 12-ton hydraulic press and metal ready for shaping.

HOW TO MAKE SILHOUETTE DIES

You can make your own dies with a jewelry saw and acrylic sheet available from a building supplier. You will need the dies to be at least ½ inch deep for the metal to deform into. Rather than buying ½-inch acrylic—which can get very expensive, is difficult to cut, and is also hard to find—I buy scrap pieces of ¼- or ⅛-inch acrylic from a hardware store and glue them together to the thickness I need.

First, cut out the design in one piece; then glue the first cutout piece to the second piece and cut out the second one along the same cut line as the first one. Continue, gluing them all together to create a ½-inch-thick piece.

Supplies

- [ ] Acrylic sheet in ¼- or ⅛-inch thickness, at least a 3-inch square
- [ ] Jewelry saw with at least a 5-inch opening
- [ ] Saw blades, size 0/2 to 0/5
- [ ] E6000 glue
- [ ] Tracing paper
- [ ] Painter's tape
- [ ] Drill press or Dremel tool
- [ ] Small drill bit
- [ ] Glue stick
- [ ] File

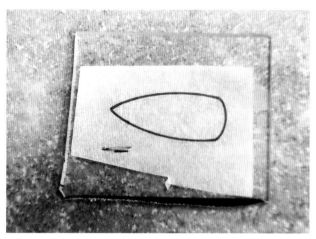

Cut enough squares of acrylic to create a depth of ½ inch. Draw your shape on a piece of tracing paper and paste it to the center of one of the acrylic squares with a glue stick, making sure you have at least a ½-inch border all the way around the outside of the acrylic to support the metal on the die. Avoid making sharp corners on your dies—curved lines are better.

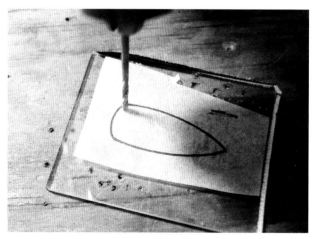

Drill a small hole on the inside of the traced line big enough to fit a saw blade through.

Cut out the acrylic along the line you drew, making sure the saw blade is not undercutting the acrylic, since this will become your template for the next piece of acrylic. Some people like to use a spiral saw blade used to cut wax, but I find I have more control using a standard jewelry saw blade to follow the lines. Use what works best for you, but don't force the saw blade or it will get stuck as the friction heats up the acrylic and break the blade.

Once you have cut out your die, use a file to smooth out any sharp edges, then use E6000 to glue the next piece to the one you just cut. Let it dry thoroughly before trying to drill and cut the next one, following the cut line from the first one. I also tape them together to help secure while cutting the next one. Continue to drill, cut, and glue until you get the correct depth of at least ½ inch.

HOW TO USE THE HYDRAULIC PRESS

Supplies

- [ ] 24-gauge dead soft annealed copper sheet
- [ ] Silhouette die
- [ ] Silicone pot holders or bicycle inner-tube pieces
- [ ] Hydraulic press
- [ ] Painter's tape
- [ ] Shears or jewelry saw

Now we are ready to use the silhouette die in the hydraulic press. Place a piece of 24-gauge dead soft copper that is not work hardened on the top of the silhouette die and secure the copper to the die with painter's tape. This keeps the copper from moving while pressing the die. If the copper has been work hardened, you will have to anneal (heat the metal with a torch to dead soft) before using it in the press.

The press comes with two steel plates. Place one of the steel plates on the bottom of the press. Lay the die with the copper on top, and place several silicone pot holders or bicycle inner-tube pieces on top of the die, followed by the second steel plate. I have found that silicone—available at kitchen stores—works really well in the press.

Lock the pressure control valve (at the bottom of the bottle jack) so that you can pump the handle on the jack. Slowly pump the handle on the jack until it gets harder to pump, then release the valve and check your die. After some experience you will know by feel just how much pressure to apply to the die.

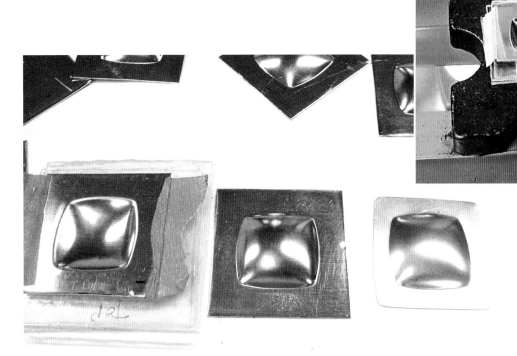

Take the completed metal out of the die and finish your piece by cutting or sawing out the shape.

Colored Pencil on Metal Technique:
Flower Pendant

The best way to show you my coloring technique is by walking you through the whole process on a piece. Let's start with a pendant with a simple flower design.

Supplies

- One 2 x 2-inch piece of 24- or 22-gauge copper sheet
- Sandpaper: grade medium 250 wet-dry and fine 650 wet-dry
- Cleanser: Bon Ami or Bar Keepers Friend
- Old toothbrush or scouring pad
- Safety glasses
- Painter's tape
- Chasing hammer
- Metal stamps
- Novacan Black Patina
- Small plastic container
- Fine steel wool
- Small sanding sponges, medium and fine grade
- Gray gesso
- Baking tin
- Heat brick

- Heat gun or hair dryer
- Heat-resistant tweezers
- #2 graphite pencil
- Soft eraser
- Extra-fine felt tip black Sharpie pen
- PrismaColor Premier colored pencils
- Clear turpentine or Turpenoid Natural
- Paintbrushes: #0 or #1 flat brush and #6 or #8 flat brush
- Two 16-gauge round jump rings, 9 mm (OD)
- 1.80 mm hole punch
- Acrylic spray
- ProtectaClear or a sealer made for metal

Instructions

doesn't bead up on the surface of the metal. Dry the metal with a paper towel and avoid touching the surface with your fingers. You can wear rubber gloves to prevent any further oils from adhering to the clean metal. You don't want any oil from your fingers to get on the surface of the metal, so handle it only at the edges. If you are stamping or texturing your piece, do it now. Tape down the metal with painter's tape to hold it in place. Don't stamp or texture over the tape or over the domed area. Mark where the jump rings will go and punch the holes.

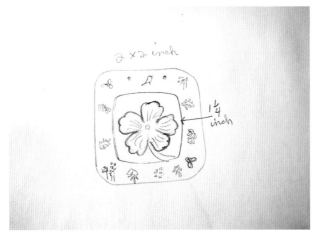

1 After shaping your metal, you are ready to start the process. On a piece of paper draw the design that you want to do in colored pencil.

3 Put some Novacan or whatever black patina you want in a glass or plastic container, and with a paintbrush paint the patina on the area that has been textured or stamped.

2 Clean the metal using a toothbrush and cleanser. The piece is clean when the water sheets off and

4 Once the piece turns black, rinse it in water and dry.

5 Using fine sandpaper, fine steel wool, or a fine sanding block, take off the excess patina to expose the textured or stamped area, sanding in one direction only. Don't worry if sanding marks or patina get on the domed area; it will soon be covered.

6 In order for the gesso to adhere to the metal, you must create a "tooth" (roughness) on the surface area that will be painted. You do this by roughing up the surface with sandpaper. Using a 1-inch piece of medium sandpaper, work in a circular motion to create a tooth for the gesso. Make sure all areas that you want gesso to stick to are sanded.

7 Squeeze a little of the gray gesso into a small cup; you will only need a few drops. Using a #6 or #8 flat brush, apply the gesso to the prepared metal. Make sure the application is smooth, and don't overload your brush with too much gesso. A thin coat is better than a thick one.

8 You will need at least two applications of gesso to cover the metal. Don't worry if the first coat doesn't cover completely and some metal shows through; the second coat will do the job. You should never need more than three coats (too many coats makes it too thick to work with). If for some reason your gesso starts to get a little too thick, just add a drop of water and shake to thin it a bit. To speed the drying time between coats, take the wet gesso piece to the heat brick and use a heat gun or hair dryer to dry each coat of gesso. Do not hold the heat source too close—about 6 inches away will do—or it will bubble. It should only take 5 or 6 seconds to dry. Use heat-safe tweezers to remove your piece from the brick and let it completely cool before applying another coat of gesso. Do not touch the piece right after using the heat gun, or you could get burned.

9 Give the piece another coat of gesso and dry it again. Clean your brush in water so the gesso doesn't dry on the brush.

10 Transfer your design with a #2 graphite pencil and a very light touch onto the gesso area, then trace the penciled lines with an extra-fine felt tip black permanent marker (a Sharpie works well).

11 With a soft eraser, take all the excess pencil lines off the gesso. The permanent pen will allow you to define the spaces between the colors.

12 You are now ready to apply colored pencil to the gray gesso. This process works similar to watercolor technique, in that you work with light colors first then darker ones. You can put a darker color on top of a lighter one but not the other way around. Color the light areas first with a light touch. Do not over-color, trying to apply too much pencil all at once, or you will start to remove the color and all that will be left is the wax from the pencil and little color.

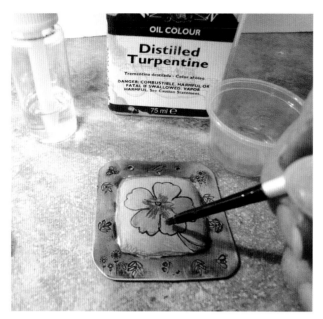

13 This is the most important step and one that will likely take some practice to master. Touch just the tip of an eyedropper into a small plastic container of turpentine or Turpenoid Natural. Do not squeeze the eyedropper onto the metal piece—just use what little is on the tip of the dropper. Using a #0 or #1 flat paintbrush, apply the turpentine or substitute to the colored pencil by dabbing it to push the colored pencil into the recesses of the gesso. Too much will make the color run and remove it. Let the piece air dry or use the heat gun to dry it.

14 Once it is dry and no longer sticky, you can add more color to any area that needs it and then repeat the turpentine process to set. Let the piece dry completely. Clean your brushes for this process with turpentine—never with water.

16 Once your piece is thoroughly dry, you can embellish the surface of the piece. I sometimes use an engraver or metal scribe to allow some of the bare metal to show through, highlighting parts of the design. Attach the jump rings.

17 Finally, you will want to use something to protect your work and keep it from tarnishing. To do this you have to protect it from the air. I have tried a lot of products, and almost all either wear off or only give short-term protection. The one product I have found that both protects the surface and is completely safe to both skin and metal is called Protecta-Clear by Everbrite, which is available on the Internet (see Resources on page 87). I have no connection to this product, but from personal experience I highly recommend it to keep your piece from interacting with your skin and to keep it from tarnishing. See Finishing Your Work on page 85 to learn more about how to seal and finish your work.

15 Once all the coloring is finished, tape off any exposed bare metal or make a template in the shape of your piece to protect the metal, then spray it with acrylic spray. Be careful to not over-spray or the color will run. It's best to use two quick sprays than one that causes the color to run. Pull off the tape and let air dry for about 10 minutes, until no longer sticky. Do not use a heat gun or the spray will melt.

Troubleshooting: Frequently Asked Questions

Q: I can see the paint strokes when I apply the gesso. What am I doing wrong?

A: You have overloaded your brush. Wipe off some of the gesso from the brush before applying more coats. If it has dried all you need to do is sand off the excess with very fine sandpaper before applying any other coats of gesso.

Q: My gesso doesn't seem to be holding to the metal. What am I doing wrong?

A: You need to make sure that you created a tooth on all areas where you will put the gesso. Gesso will flake or peel off bare, untextured metal.

Q: When I applied the gesso and dried my piece, the gesso bubbled. What went wrong and how do I fix it?

A: You were holding the heat gun a little too close to your work and the heat caused it to bubble. Let your piece thoroughly dry and then use fine sandpaper to smooth out the bubble. Do another coat of gesso if needed.

Q: When I applied the patina to the stamped edges it got on the area where I want to apply the gesso. Is this a problem?

A: No, it will not be a problem. The gesso will adhere to the metal with the patina on it.

Q: It seems that the color is just laying on the top of the gesso and it isn't covering very well.

A: Don't worry! The first coat doesn't cover well. Once you use a little turpentine, it will blend into the gesso.

Q: It seems that the more color I try to put on the less color I see on my piece. What is happening?

A: This is because your piece has become saturated with too much wax from the colored pencil. Gently remove some of the wax buildup with your small paintbrush and a little turpentine and let it dry before applying more colored pencil.

Q: I don't like the color I applied. Can I remove it?

A: Yes, as long as it isn't all over the whole piece. Use turpentine in small amounts to remove the color. Let it dry before applying more color.

Q: When I applied the turpentine, the color ran. What am I doing wrong?

A: You are applying too much turpentine to the surface of the color. You only need a brush barely damp to blend the color into the gesso. Also only use a very small #0 or #1 flat brush, which will help with not getting too much turpentine on your piece. Less is always more when it comes to using the turpentine.

Q: After using the turpentine my piece is sticky and it doesn't seem to dry.

A: You used too much turpentine to blend the color. Your brush barely needs to be damp to get the color to blend. It takes longer to dry when it is damp out or raining so keep this in mind when working on your piece. You may need to let it dry for a day or two before continuing to add more color or seal.

Q: I pushed too hard when applying the black Sharpie pen and exposed the copper. What should I do?

A: Just take a little gesso and touch it up in the area that is exposed and let it dry completely before reapplying the black Sharpie pen. You can also use your micro engraver or sharp metal scribe to make the mark a highlight.

Q: Every time I try to use the colored pencils on the gesso it takes off the gesso down to the bare metal.

A: Several things could be happening. Either the gesso isn't completely dry, the gesso was too thick when applied, or you are pushing too hard on the pencils.

Cheat Sheet

The Cheat Sheet summarizes the steps used in the coloring process. It will help you to follow the correct steps without having to reread every detail of the process.

1. Draw your design on a piece of paper.

2. Shape your metal.

3. Sand the area that will have gesso applied.

4. Mark where your jump ring(s) will go and punch the hole(s).

5. Clean the metal.

6. If your piece is going to be stamped or textured, do it now.

7. Apply patina and sand off excess.

8. Apply gesso and dry. Repeat for a total of two coats.

9. Transfer your design to the gesso using a light touch with a pencil.

10. Trace penciled lines with your extra-fine Sharpie pen.

11. Color your piece.

12. Blend with turpentine and let dry. Color and repeat turpentine.

13. Tape off exposed metal not colored and spray with acrylic and let dry.

14. Highlight with micro engraver.

15. Attach jump rings.

16. Seal whole piece with ProtectaClear or a sealer made for metal.

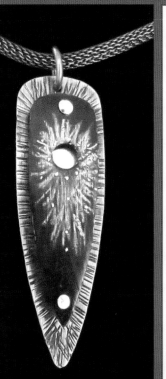

Projects Using the Colored Pencil Technique

In this section of the book you will learn several techniques using Premier PrismaColor pencils. Some require using a solvent to blend the colors; others will only use the colored pencils alone giving a totally different effect. You can explore your own way to work with these wonderful colored pencils as well. The projects are meant to be simple enough for a beginner to do and also allow the more experienced metalworker a way to add to their own work.

Heart of My Heart Pendant

This <u>heart</u> is done without shaping on a hydraulic press and is easy for anyone to do with few tools. Using a single color allows you to learn how to blend and work the colored pencils before moving on to more complicated designs.

Supplies

- [ ] Two 3 x 3-inch pieces of 22- or 24-gauge copper sheet
- [ ] Jewelry saw or metal shears
- [ ] Chasing hammer
- [ ] Riveting hammer
- [ ] Medium and fine sandpaper
- [ ] Fine steel wool
- [ ] Two .05-inch or 1.27 mm copper rivets (available from Rio Grande)
- [ ] Flush cutters
- [ ] Safety glasses
- [ ] 1.25 mm hole punch or drill bit to fit the rivets and 1.80 mm punch for jump ring holes
- [ ] PrismaColor Premier colored pencils
- [ ] Tracing paper
- [ ] Gesso
- [ ] Turpentine
- [ ] Acrylic spray
- [ ] Scribe or engraver
- [ ] Small #1 and #8 flat brushes
- [ ] 1 mm or 2 mm dimple pliers or punch
- [ ] Two 16-gauge round jump rings, 9 mm (OD)
- [ ] Novacan Black Patina
- [ ] ProtectaClear or a sealer made for metal

Instructions

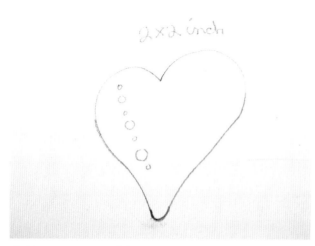

1 Draw a 2 x 2-inch heart on a piece of paper and use this to make your heart by copying the heart onto a piece of tracing paper and gluing the tracing paper to one of the 3 x 3 sheets of copper.

2 Using a saw or metal shears, cut out your heart (or use a pancake die to cut a heart). File and sand the edges till they are smooth. Rough up the surface on the front of the heart with medium sandpaper, then use dimple pliers or punch to place the design down the left side of your heart as shown on the finished heart. Clean the piece to remove any oils or dirt from your hands, and let it dry.

3 Apply two coats of gesso to the heart and dry with a heat gun or hair dryer. Using a dark red or maroon pencil, color the edges of the heart as shown. Use a lighter red to color the whole heart. Don't worry if it doesn't look completely covered, since this is only the first coat. Apply a very small amount of turpentine to a brush and dab it onto the heart, pushing the color into the gesso.

4 This is what it looks like after the first coloring and application of turpentine. Once it is dry, apply another coat of color to the heart.

5 The second coat of color should cover all the gesso. Allow the piece to dry thoroughly before spraying with acrylic.

6 Put your heart on a piece of paper or cardboard and spray outdoors. Spray a light coat of acrylic on the heart and let dry.

7 Using an engraver or metal scribe, highlight the dimpled areas and add spirals and dots. Punch a hole in the upper right-hand side of the heart as shown. If this is your completed piece, put a jump ring in the hole and add a chain.

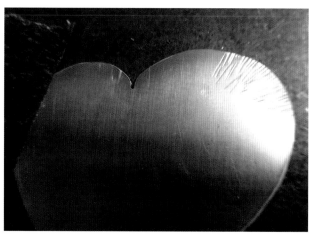

10 Using a texturing or riveting hammer, hammer all around the outside of the heart. While hammering, the heart may buckle. Turn it over and use a mallet to flatten the metal as you go.

8 If you want to add the background piece, draw and cut another heart—this one 2½ x 2½ inches—on the second 3 x 3-inch sheet of copper. This will create a ¼-inch edge around the colored heart that you just finished. File and sand the edges.

11 Check to make sure that the finished heart will cover the inside ends of the marks when done hammering.

9 Place your colored heart on the second heart to check the size. It should have a fairly even ¼-inch edge around all sides.

12 Clean your heart with a cleanser such as Bar Keepers Friend. Once water runs off without beading up on the surface of the heart, it is clean and ready for patina. Be careful not to touch anything but the edges so you don't get any oil on your piece.

14 Center your colored heart over the bigger heart and mark the hole on the top with a Sharpie pen using the hole created on the first heart. This will become the hole for the first rivet. Mark the hole for the second rivet as shown. Punch the second hole on the mark where the second rivet will go.

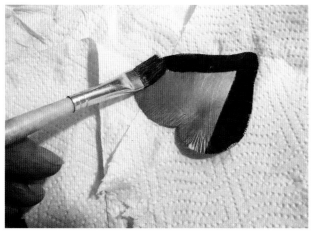

13 Use a clean brush to apply whatever dark patina solution you want around the hammered edge. I used Novacan Black Patina. Once the piece turns black, rinse in water and dry. Highlight your piece by cleaning off the excess patina with fine sandpaper or fine steel wool.

15 Punch the top hole that you marked on the second heart. Wearing safety glasses place the rivet in the holes on both hearts from the front, then cut the rivet on the back with the flush cutters to 2 mm and set the rivet from the back of the piece using a chasing hammer. Mark the second hole and move the heart to the side so you can punch the second hole on the bottom piece. Do not punch the bottom hole till the first rivet is set.

16 Move the heart back in place and set the second rivet from the back using a chasing hammer.

17 Now that both rivets are set, punch a hole on the outer heart above the top rivet as shown and insert a jump ring if you want your piece to hang from just one ring.

18 If you want your heart to hang from a chain, make another hole on the other side of the heart and insert the second jump ring.

19 Seal the finished piece with ProtectaClear or a metal sealer.

Waves of Blue Pendant

This is another piece created without the use of a hydraulic press, so it is easy for anyone to make. This project teaches how to work with more than one color and how to highlight with a micro engraver.

Supplies

- ☐ One 2 x 1-inch piece of 22- or 24-gauge copper sheet
- ☐ One 2½ x 1½-inch piece of 22- or 24-gauge copper sheet
- ☐ Jewelry saw or metal shears
- ☐ Chasing hammer
- ☐ Gesso
- ☐ Extra-fine felt tip black Sharpie pen
- ☐ Two .05-inch or 1.27 mm copper rivets (available from Rio Grande)
- ☐ 1.25 mm hole punch or drill bit to fit the rivets and 1.80 mm punch for jump ring holes
- ☐ PrismaColor Premier colored pencils
- ☐ Tracing paper and graphite paper
- ☐ #2 graphite pencil
- ☐ Soft eraser
- ☐ Scribe or engraver
- ☐ Turpentine
- ☐ Small #1 and #8 flat brushes
- ☐ Two 16-gauge round jump rings, 9 mm (OD)
- ☐ Novacan Black Patina
- ☐ Medium and fine sandpaper or fine steel wool
- ☐ Safety glasses
- ☐ Flush cutters
- ☐ ProtectaClear or a sealer made for metal

Instructions

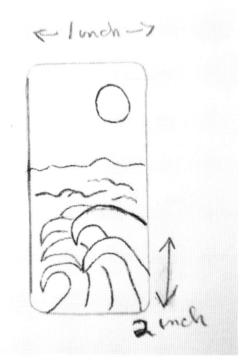

2 Using an extra-fine felt tip black Sharpie pen, trace over all the lines, then erase all the graphite lines with a soft eraser.

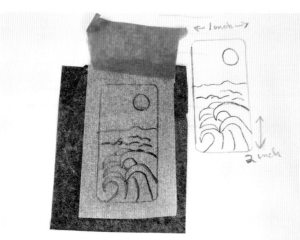

3 Apply the first layer of colored pencil on the entire piece, blend with turpentine, and dry.

1 Sand and file all edges of the 2 x 1-inch piece of copper listed in the supply list. Using medium sandpaper create a tooth for the gesso, then apply two coats of gesso, drying well between each coat. Copy the design using tracing paper, then place a piece of graphite paper under the tracing paper and on top of the copper to transfer the design to the gesso, or transfer the design to the gesso with a pencil.

4 Continue to add more color to your piece as shown, then blend with turpentine and dry.

5 After all the coloring is done, spray your work with the acrylic spray and air dry until it is no longer tacky. Using a scribe or engraver, highlight some of the areas as shown.

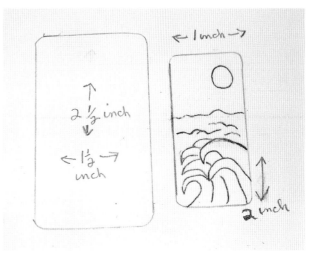

6 File and sand all edges of the 2 ½ x 1 ½-inch piece of copper. Make sure the colored piece of copper fits nicely inside the larger piece. Clean the larger piece until water sheets off and doesn't bead up. Don't touch the area that has been cleaned.

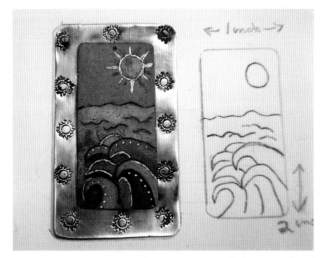

7 Texture or use metal stamps around the outside of the larger piece of copper, then apply black patina. Let dry and clean up excess patina. Mark and punch for the two rivets on the colored piece only.

metal stamps

8 Place your colored piece in the center of the textured piece and mark where the top rivet will go by marking though the hole you already punched. Wearing safety glasses, put the rivets through the front, then cut the rivet to 2 mm and set it from the back. It will be a tight fit, so use a chasing hammer to tap the rivet through the hole. Mark where the bottom rivet will go by marking through the punched hole on the colored piece. Punch the bottom hole and set the second rivet.

9 Mark and punch two holes for the jump rings. Place the jump rings through the holes in your finished piece.

Geometric Design Pendant

If you are daunted by the idea of drawing a design, this project uses only simple lines, circles, and spirals to create a beautiful colored pencil piece. This piece was made with a silhouette die but can be done on a flat piece as well.

Supplies

- [ ] One 3 x 3-inch piece of 22- or 24-gauge copper sheet
- [ ] Silhouette die **?**
- [ ] Jewelry saw or metal shears
- [ ] Safety glasses
- [ ] Riveting hammer
- [ ] 1.5 mm or 1.8 mm hole punch or drill bit
- [ ] PrismaColor Premier colored pencils
- [ ] Gesso
- [ ] #2 graphite pencil
- [ ] Soft eraser
- [ ] Medium and fine sandpaper or fine steel wool
- [ ] Scribe or engraver
- [ ] Turpentine
- [ ] Small #1 and #8 flat brushes
- [ ] 1 mm or 2 mm dimple pliers or punch
- [ ] One 16-gauge round jump ring, 9 mm (OD)
- [ ] Novacan Black Patina
- [ ] ProtectaClear or a sealer made for metal

Instructions

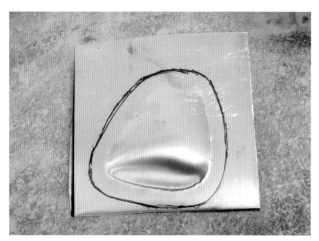

1 Use a silhouette die to create a 1¾ x 2-inch domed area, then draw a ¼-inch edge around the domed copper with a Sharpie pen so the finished piece will be 2 x 2¼ inches as shown. Cut out your piece, and file and sand the edges.

2 Trace the die onto a piece of paper as shown and create the design.

3 Using medium sandpaper create the tooth on the domed area only. Mark and punch a hole at the top for the jump ring with a 1.5 mm or 1.8 mm punch. Clean your piece thoroughly before texturing and using the dimple pliers on the edges, being careful not to dent the domed area. Patina just the edges, then rinse and dry your piece.

4 Use fine sandpaper or fine steel wool to remove just enough of the patina to show contrast.

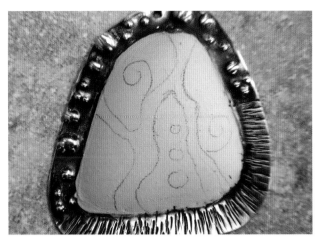

5 Apply two coats of gesso to the domed area only and dry with the heat gun or hair dryer. Transfer the design with a pencil to the gesso.

6 Trace all lines with the extra-fine felt tip black Sharpie pen and remove any pencil lines with a soft eraser.

7 Apply the first layer of colored pencil, blend with turpentine, and dry.

8 Apply the second layer of colored pencil, blend with turpentine, and dry.

9 After all the coloring is done, tape off the bare metal with painter's tape and spray with the acrylic spray. Once the spray is completely dry, use a scribe or engraver to highlight as shown. Attach the jump ring.

10 Seal your piece with ProtectaClear or a metal sealer.

Tree of Life Pendant

Who doesn't love trees? They are extremely popular and also fairly easy to draw. This project allows you to try out your drawing skills and work with lots of colors. It is also a good project for those just starting to use a hydraulic press and jewelry saw.

Supplies

- [ ] One 3 x 3-inch piece of 24-gauge copper sheet
- [ ] Extra-fine felt tip black Sharpie pen
- [ ] Jewelry saw and saw blades, size 0/4
- [ ] Safety glasses
- [ ] Novacan Black Patina
- [ ] 1.5 mm hole punch
- [ ] Medium and fine sandpaper or fine steel wool
- [ ] Gray gesso
- [ ] #2 graphite pencil
- [ ] Soft eraser
- [ ] PrismaColor Premier colored pencils
- [ ] Turpentine
- [ ] Small #1 and #8 flat brushes
- [ ] Acrylic spray
- [ ] Scribe or engraver
- [ ] Two 16-gauge round jump rings, 9 mm (OD)
- [ ] ProtectaClear or a sealer made for metal

Instructions

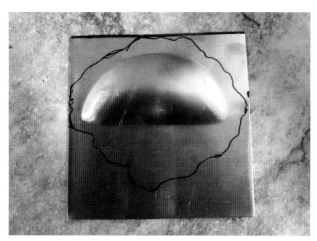

1 Using a hydraulic press, create a half-moon domed shape on the upper portion of the 3 x 3-inch piece of copper. The domed part should be 2½ x 1½ inches. Using an extra-fine felt tip black Sharpie pen, draw your outer shape. If you want to use a flat piece of copper, mark the half-moon shape on the copper and the outer shape now.

2 Using a jewelry saw, cut out the shape, then file and sand the edges until smooth.

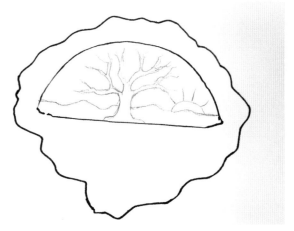

3 Trace the shape onto a piece of paper and create the tree design, keeping in mind not to use too many lines; in other words, leave space for coloring. Keeping your design simple will produce a better finished piece.

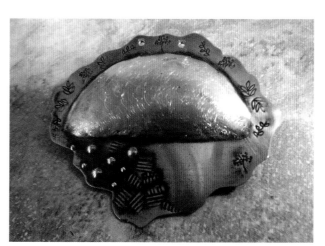

4 Mark where the two jump rings will go and punch the holes. Clean your piece before stamping the outer edges, making sure to leave some unstamped parts for negative space. Patina only the stamped area with black Novacan or another black patina. Rinse, dry, and use fine steel wool or fine sandpaper to remove the excess patina. Create a tooth on the area to receive gesso with medium sandpaper, rubbing in a circular motion.

5 Apply two coats of gray gesso, drying well between coats.

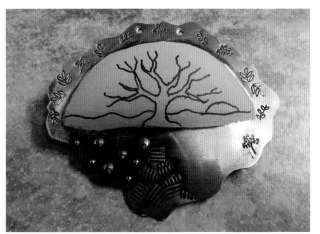

6 Transfer your design to the gesso area using a pencil with a light touch, then go over all the lines with an extra-fine felt tip black Sharpie pen. Remove any pencil lines with a soft eraser. Don't worry if your tree isn't exactly like the one in your original design—remember nature doesn't like straight lines. Curves are much more interesting and will make for a better design.

7 Apply the first layer of colored pencil on the entire piece, blend with turpentine, dry, and repeat if necessary. Spray only the colored area with acrylic spray.

8 Once your piece is no longer tacky from the acrylic spray and completely dry, use an engraver or metal scribe to highlight some of the areas as shown. Remember that you only want to remove the colored pencil but not the metal itself, so a light touch is needed with the engraver. Spray the colored portion again with acrylic to protect the metal area that has been etched or it will tarnish. Attach the jump rings, then seal the pendant with ProtectaClear or a metal sealer.

Fourth of July Pendant

This project works with black gesso, which gives a lot of contrast with the colored pencils. There is no blending of the colors or use of turpentine. This allows for the gesso to show through as an element in the piece. This pendant is a little more complex since it uses small tubes to raise the piece for more dimension.

Supplies

- [ ] One 3 x 2-inch 24-gauge copper sheet
- [ ] One 2 x 1-inch 24-gauge copper sheet
- [ ] ³⁄₁₆-inch large hole punch, or jewelry saw
- [ ] Shears or jewelry saw and saw blades, size 0/4
- [ ] Flush cutters — ?
- [ ] Safety glasses — set
- [ ] One 16-gauge round jump ring, 9 mm (OD)
- [ ] Riveting hammer ?
- [ ] One 2.35 mm copper or brass tube — ?
- [ ] Two 18 x ½-inch brass finishing nails
- [ ] 1.25 mm and 1.80 mm hole punch
- [ ] Scribe or engraver —
- [ ] Medium and fine sandpaper
- [ ] Fine steel wool
- [ ] Novacan Black Patina
- [ ] Black gesso
- [ ] ProtectaClear or a sealer made for metal

Instructions

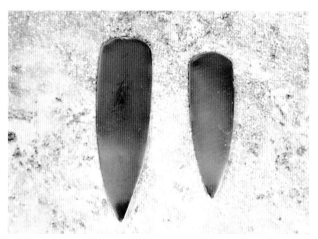

1 Cut one piece of copper 2 inches long by 1 1/16 inches wide and one piece 1 1/2 inches long by 1/2 inch wide, tapering to a point as shown.

2 The smaller piece should fit nicely on top of the larger piece.

3 Cut a 3/16-inch hole one-third of the way from the top of the smaller piece and create a tooth with medium sandpaper on the front where the gesso will go. Mark and punch for the rivets on the smaller piece as shown with a 1.25 mm hole punch.

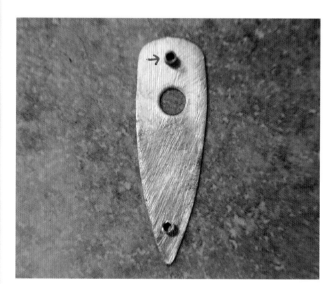

4 Cut two pieces of tubing to 2.5 mm long using a tube cutter and a jewelry saw; these will be the spacers between the top and bottom of the piece.

5 Wearing safety glasses, use a riveting hammer to make hash marks all the way around the edge of the bigger piece. Clean the piece thoroughly, then add patina. Rinse, dry, and use fine sandpaper to remove the excess patina. Seal this piece with ProtectaClear or a metal sealer before going on to the next piece, as it will be difficult to access after the piece is finished.

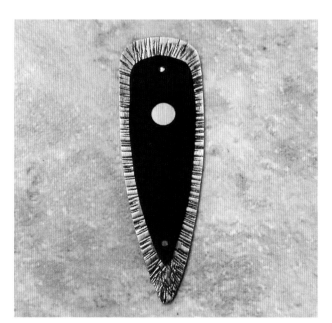

6 Paint two coats of black gesso on the sanded smaller piece and dry well. Mark where the holes will be for the rivets on the larger piece as shown by matching up the holes on the smaller piece. Use the 1.25 mm hole punch to cut the holes.

7 Turn the gesso piece over and place the small tubes over the nail rivets as shown. It will be a tight fit, so you may have to hammer the finishing nails through the piece then put on the tubes.

8 Place the larger piece with the patina side down on top of the tubes and finishing nails as shown. Cut the first finishing nail to about 2 mm with flush cutters and use a chasing hammer to rivet to the back, then do the second nail.

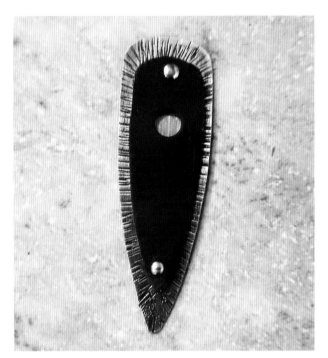

9 Turn your riveted piece over and touch up any areas where the gesso may have come off; let dry.

10 Using the colored pencils, draw a starburst around the hole you created at the top. There is no need to use turpentine on this project. Use a scribe or micro engraver to highlight the starburst with dots as shown. Punch a hole at the top and place the jump ring. Seal the rest of the piece with ProtectaClear or a metal sealer.

Blooming Flowers Bracelet

This project is the most complex of all the ones in this book. It may be a challenge for the beginner, but the coloring technique is easy to do and can be applied to other projects if you are not quite ready for this one.

Supplies

- [ ] One 2 x 2-inch 24-gauge copper sheet
- [ ] Two 1¼-inch 24-gauge copper sheets
- [ ] One 6 x 1-inch 21- or 24-gauge copper bracelet blank
- [ ] Four .05 inch or 1.27 mm copper rivets, or 18 x ½-inch brass finishing nails
- [ ] Bracelet mandrel or rolling pin
- [ ] Chasing hammer
- [ ] Medium and fine sandpaper
- [ ] Mallet
- [ ] Scribe or engraver
- [ ] Flush cutters
- [ ] Gray gesso
- [ ] Turpentine
- [ ] Round-nose pliers
- [ ] Tracing paper
- [ ] PrismaColor Premier colored pencils
- [ ] Acrylic spray
- [ ] Safety glasses
- [ ] Shears or jewelry saw
- [ ] Novacan Black Patina
- [ ] 1.25 mm or 1.5 mm long-neck hole punch or 1.32 mm drill bit to fit rivets
- [ ] ProtectaClear or a sealer made for metal

Instructions

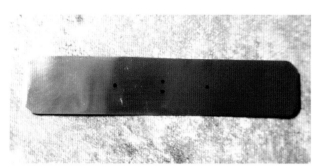

1 Shape the ends of the bracelet blank by cutting off the edges; curve them with a file and sand smooth. Using a chasing hammer, distress the surface of the bracelet. Clean with cleanser to remove all oil from the blank, making sure that the water sheets off and does not bead up. Dry, patina, rinse, and sand off excess patina. Mark the center at 3 inches from the end with two marks one above the other ⅛ inch apart. Mark 1 inch from the center on both sides for holes and punch with the 1.25 mm hole punch or 1.32 mm drill bit.

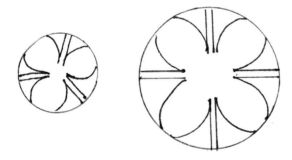

2 Copy the flower template to size (1¼-inch circle and 1¾-inch circle).

3 Trace the large flower to tracing paper using a 1¾-inch template circle and paste with a glue stick to the 2-inch copper. Do the same for both smaller 1¼-inch flower circles.

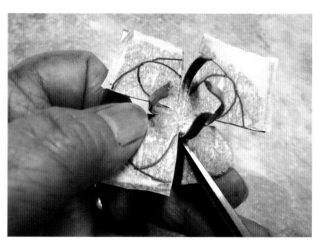

4 Wearing safety glasses, cut the large flower's straight lines first with either metal shears or a jewelry saw. Once you have cut the straight lines, pull them up and out of the way so you can cut the petals.

5 Remove the tracing paper from the copper by soaking in water, then dry and file all flowers to shape and remove any burrs. Flatten all flowers as shown.

6 Use medium sandpaper to create a tooth on one side of the flowers but not the stamens. Punch the two holes to match up with the bracelet in the center of the large flower with the long-nose 1.5 mm hole punch or drill bit. With the rivets in place, use the flush cutter to cut rivets to 2 mm and rivet the copper or brass rivets to the bracelet on the back. The two rivets keep the flower from turning while wearing. Punch the holes on the smaller flowers and rivet in place. Make sure to use safety glasses.

7 Do not worry that the flowers seem too close together. Place the bracelet on the bracelet mandrel and shape it using a plastic mallet, and the flowers will spread as shown.

8 Once your bracelet has been shaped on the mandrel to the proper size, you can shape all the petals, carefully pulling them up into place and using round pliers to shape the petals.

9 With all the petals in place and shaped, it is now time to apply gesso.

10 Apply two coats of gesso to only the flowers, not the stamens, and let dry before starting to apply the color.

11 Apply the first coat of color with the colored pencils.

12 Blend the color into the gesso with turpentine. Let dry.

13 Apply more color as needed.

14 To protect the bare metal on the bracelet blank, put pieces of paper under and around the flowers before spraying them with acrylic spray.

15 After the spray is dry, turn down all the stamens with round-nose pliers as shown. Highlight flowers if desired with an engraver or scribe. Seal the entire bracelet with ProtectaClear or a metal sealer.

Other Coloring Techniques, Patinas, and Finishing

There are many ways to color metal that will produce an interesting effect on copper by adding depth and texture to your work. One of these is patina, which is just a fancy name for tarnish, oxidation, and the natural aging process on metal. We can hasten the process by using commercial chemicals (as we've described earlier) or things you have around the house already, such as salt and vinegar or just plain heat. Patina makes a nice base for applying colored pencil.

Remember to first clean the metal to remove all oils and tarnish before applying any patina on the raw copper or the patina will not work. I like to use Bon Ami or Bar Keepers Friend with a small brush or scouring pad to clean metal. You can wear rubber gloves to prevent any further oils from adhering to the clean metal. The metal is clean when the water sheets off and doesn't bead up.

Green Commercial Patina

Green patina works nicely on copper and brass. There are several commercial patinas that work well. When working with any patina, it is best to do it in a well-ventilated area and at room temperature. With any patina, no two applications will come out the same, so don't try to control it. Let the patina happen as it will, and stop the process when you reach an effect you like.

Jax and Sculpt Nouveau are two commercially ready-to-use green patinas that are easy and safe to use. Follow the manufacturer's directions for best results.

This heart has been textured and is ready for an application of Jax Green Patina.

One application of Jax Green Patina was used as the base for the colored pencil on the heart to highlight the textured surface. The heart was then riveted onto a piece of heat-treated patina copper and sprayed with ProtectaClear to seal the color and keep it from further tarnishing.

Salt and Vinegar Patina:
Green Jewel of the Nile Pendant

This is another method to get a green patina on copper. It allows the fumes of the salt and vinegar to slowly develop on the surface of the copper while suspended over the solution on the bottom of the bowl.

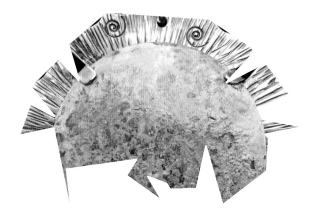

Supplies

- [ ] One 1 ½-inch round 24-gauge copper disc
- [ ] One 2-inch round 24-gauge copper disc
- [ ] One 16-gauge round jump ring, 9 mm (OD)
- [ ] Jewelry saw and saw blades, size 0/4
- [ ] Safety glasses
- [ ] Medium and fine sandpaper
- [ ] Fine steel wool
- [ ] Plastic or glass container
- [ ] Non-iodine salt (kosher salt)
- [ ] White vinegar
- [ ] Paper towels
- [ ] Wire coat hanger
- [ ] Bezel pusher ▬
- [ ] Dap
- [ ] Dapping block ▬
- [ ] 1.80 mm hole punch

A salt and vinegar patina is an easy way to get a nice green-blue patina on copper. It takes a while to develop the color, and you can never be quite sure what the result will be, but it is always worth the wait.

Instructions

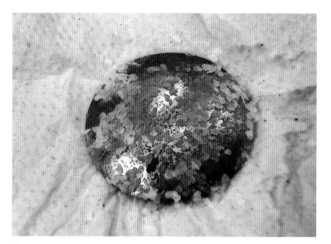

2 Dissolve equal amounts of salt and vinegar in a glass or plastic bowl with a lid (don't worry if not all the salt dissolves). Completely cover your piece and soak in the solution for 30 minutes. Remove and let air dry. Suspend the piece over the dish with the salt and vinegar by using a coat hanger so it sits in the center. Sprinkle a little of the salt and vinegar solution on it before putting the lid on the bowl. It will take from a few hours to several days to get a good patina.

1 Dap the 1½-inch copper disc in a large-hole dapping block, then sand the copper round with 250 sandpaper to give it a little tooth to help the patina stick to the surface. Clean your piece so there is no oil or dirt on the surface, until the water sheets off the piece, and dry.

3 After 6 hours little color has developed, so back in the bowl for more time.

4 After 24 hours the color has developed, so very lightly rinse off the excess salt. This piece still needs more time.

5 Wet a piece of paper towel in the solution and place on the suspended piece; let stand until the color develops some more.

6 Here it is at another 3 hours. Carefully pick off any excess salt and let dry. (I use a hair dryer to speed up drying.) Do not rinse the piece at this point as it will remove too much of the patina.

7 After the patina is developed and the piece is dry, I use colored pencils to enhance and fill in some of the color right over the patina. Seal your piece with acrylic spray or ProtectaClear.

8 Place the colored piece in the center of the 2-inch copper disc and use an extra-fine felt tip black Sharpie pen to trace the 1 ½-inch colored piece so that it is centered on the larger disc. Mark the top where the jump ring will go and where the four approximately 2.75 mm-wide prongs will be as shown. Draw around the 2-inch disc with the pen, making an uneven edge.

10 Make sure your piece fits nicely in the center before cutting the prongs to about 4 mm. File and shape the prongs, then cut the hole for the jump ring.

9 Cut the prongs up to the inner line with a jewelry saw and pull up the prongs before cutting the curved outer edge. File, sand, and smooth all edges.

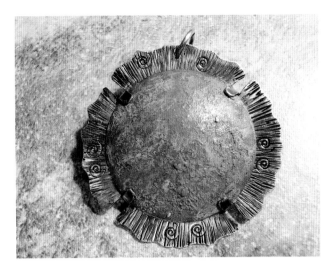

11 Using a metal stamp or texturing hammer, stamp the edge of the 2-inch disc, then clean and dry thoroughly. Apply Novacan Black Patina, rinse, and dry. Sand with fine sandpaper or fine steel wool to highlight the edge. Lay your colored piece on the disc and set the prongs by pushing them over with a bezel pusher; put on the jump ring. Seal the whole piece with ProtectaClear or a metal sealer.

Salt and Ammonia Patina: Celestial Spiral Pendant

Salt and ammonia patina is easy to do and gives a bluish patina to copper. This is not an exact science so be patient and be amazed with what you end up creating.

Supplies

- [ ] One 1 ½-inch round 24-gauge copper disc
- [ ] One 2-inch round 24-gauge copper disc
- [ ] One 16-gauge round jump ring, 9 mm (OD)
- [ ] 1.80 mm hole punch
- [ ] Jewelry saw and saw blades, size 0/4
- [ ] Safety glasses
- [ ] Medium and fine sandpaper
- [ ] Fine steel wool
- [ ] Plastic container with lid
- [ ] Small plastic yogurt container
- [ ] Small 4-ounce spray bottle
- [ ] Non-iodine salt (kosher salt)
- [ ] Non-sudsy white household ammonia
- [ ] Paper towels
- [ ] Wire coat hanger
- [ ] Scribe or engraver
- [ ] Bezel pusher
- [ ] Dap
- [ ] Dapping block

Instructions

1 Dap the 1½-inch copper disc in a large-hole dapping block, then sand the copper round with 250 sandpaper to give it a little tooth to help the patina stick to the surface. Clean the sanded side with cleanser to get any oil off the piece. Be careful not to touch the surface once clean.

2 Mix 3 ounces of warm water with as much salt as will dissolve in the small spray bottle. Spray the copper piece with the salt water and let dry a little before sprinkling more salt over it.

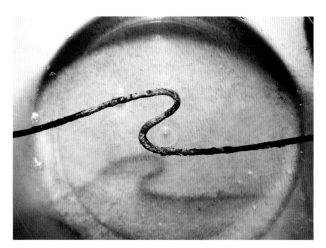

3 Cut the coat hanger wire so it fits across the top of the plastic container, then cut a notch in both sides of the container so the wire can rest just below the lid.

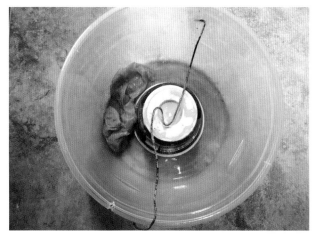

4 Place an ammonia-soaked paper towel in the bottom of the plastic container, then place the small plastic yogurt container upside down in the middle of the container. Now you can either hang a bracelet or suspend the piece of copper over the top of the yogurt container. Put the lid on the container and watch the patina develop. It could take as little as a few minutes or as much as a few days to get the desired patina.

5 Once your piece is ready, remove it from the container and let dry before carefully shaking off the excess salt. Some of the patina will come off with the salt. If too much comes off, just re-spray lightly with the salt water, sprinkle with salt, and place back in the container to develop again.

Once the patina has developed, I use colored pencils to enhance and fill in some of the color right over the patina. Seal your piece with acrylic spray or ProtectaClear.

6 Place your colored piece in the center of the 2-inch copper disc and use an extra-fine felt tip black Sharpie pen to trace the 1½-inch colored piece so that it is centered on the larger disc. Mark the top where the jump ring will go and where the four approximately 2.75 mm-wide prongs will be as shown. Draw around the 2-inch disc with the pen, making an uneven edge.

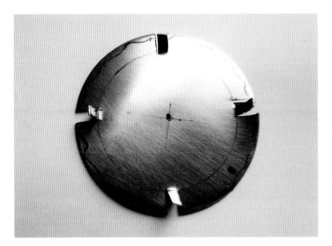

7 Cut the prongs up to the inner line with a jewelry saw and pull up the prongs before cutting the curved outer edge. File, sand, and smooth all edges.

8 Make sure your piece fits nicely in the center before cutting the prongs to about 4 mm. File and shape the prongs, then cut the hole for the jump ring.

9 Using a metal stamp or texturing hammer, stamp the edge of the 2-inch disc, then clean and dry thoroughly. Apply Novacan Black Patina, rinse, and dry. Sand with fine sandpaper or fine steel wool to highlight the edge. Lay your colored piece on the disc and set the prongs by pushing them over with a bezel pusher; put on the jump ring. Seal the whole piece with ProtectaClear or a metal sealer.

Miracle-Gro Formula

This is one of my favorite formulas for a blue-green patina. I love the color it develops and it is faster than the other methods, as well.

Mix equal amounts of vinegar and Miracle-Gro. Place the metal in the mixture and allow the patina to develop. Remove the piece and allow it to air dry. You can also try mixing Miracle-Gro with water for a more intensely blue patina. Seal the patina with ProtectaClear or a metal sealer.

Another example of a Miracle-Gro patina.

Heat Patina

Heat patina is fun and easy to do with a small torch. You never know what you will get; colors range from gold, orange, pink, and purple to dark blue, light blue, and black. All you need is a piece of copper.

Start by heating the piece slowly, then go in a little closer and quickly take the flame away and watch the color form as it cools. Just play with it till you get what you like. If you overheat your piece you will not get very pretty colors. If you don't get what you like, let it cool, clean the metal, and do it again. Sometimes the color on the back of your piece is as pretty as the front.

Supplies

- [ ] Copper piece to tarnish
- [ ] Solder brick or heat-safe surface
- [ ] Small micro torch
- [ ] Heat-safe tweezers
- [ ] Container of cool water
- [ ] ProtectaClear or a sealer made for metal

Instructions

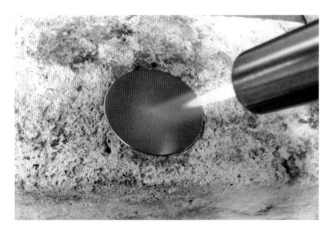

1 Put the piece of copper on a solder brick or heat-safe surface and start to heat it with the torch. As it heats, move the flame around, as this creates different shapes.

2 As the copper starts to get some color, move to another area of the piece. I like to get close then quickly remove the flame to see what colors I am getting.

3 At this point don't go back to the areas you just did or you will lose the color.

4 Keep moving to unheated areas to complete the color, then quickly put the piece in water to cool it down so you don't lose the color.

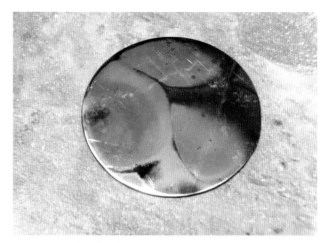

5 This is the finished piece. You will need to seal it or it will continue to tarnish; some colors may change once you seal your piece because the oxide is only on the surface of the metal. It will change and lose some of the color. The best way to try and keep as much of the color as possible is to spray it with a very light coat of ProtectaClear and let dry, then spray another light coat to finish. You can also try Renaissance Wax, but even this will not keep all the color.

Just applying heat from a small torch can add a surprising and lovely patina to copper.

A nice way to use heat patina is on a background piece for a metal silhouette.

Gilders Paste

Baroque Art Gilders Paste is similar to old-fashioned waxy shoe polish. This stuff can add great highlights to your colored pencil work, hide imperfections, and bring new life to older work.

This ginkgo leaf was treated with a salt and ammonia patina. This is what it looks like before applying Gilders Paste. One nice thing about patina is that you can add colored pencil directly to any areas that need a little more color.

I used Gilders Paste and Inka-Gold on this leaf after I sprayed it with ProtectaClear.

On this leaf I used dark blue Gilders Paste on the edge and gold on the surface to bring out some contrast on an otherwise dull-looking piece.

Finishing Your Work

I really have a thing about sloppy work. Take the time to clean up your work as you go. Clean and polish both the front and back of your piece. Do it right the first time and you will not have to come back and clean it up later. Close your eyes and run your fingers all over your piece. If you can feel any burrs, use a file or sandpaper to remove them. Use your sense of feel as much as your eyes to check your finished work.

Working with copper, brass, and even sterling silver is a challenge when it comes to tarnish. Keeping your work looking the same as when you first made it presents a real problem. Your work will continue to tarnish and need continual cleaning to keep it looking good unless you coat it with something that will stop the tarnishing.

I have tried many products to keep my work looking good. Renaissance Wax works for a little while but doesn't stop the tarnish from coming back, and the wax attracts dirt. Sprays and varnishes turn yellow or peel off, leaving your pieces looking worse than if you did nothing.

The one product I found that does work is Protecta-Clear by Everbrite. It stops tarnish and preserves patina, protects sensitive skin from metals and stops skin discoloration, and is practically invisible. ProtectaClear will not crack or yellow like lacquers or acrylics, and the coating remains flexible so you can use it on bracelets.

I highly recommend this product and have never used anything better. I have no financial connection to the company—I just love the product. For more information on where to purchase it, see Resources on page 87.

ProtectaClear comes in both liquid and spray form. Both work well, and I use both. Once you have finished your piece and sprayed just the colored portion with acrylic spray and it has been dry for at least a day, you can apply the ProtectaClear. Wearing nitrile or chemical gloves, clean the bare metal with denatured alcohol before applying the ProtectaClear. I use Q-tips and alcohol to thoroughly clean any oil, dirt, or polishing compounds off any bare metal on my pieces. Always work in a well-ventilated area or outside.

I use a natural soft art brush to apply the liquid to just one side at a time, being careful not to put too much on or it will drip. It is better to apply two thinner coats than one coat that runs. You can apply it over the colored portion of your piece, but again be careful, as too much can make the color run. This is where the spray form of ProtectaClear works best, but watch that you don't over-spray. The product will dry to the touch in about 15 minutes but needs several days to cure. You should not need more than two coats to adequately protect your work.

RESOURCES

These are many of the resources that I use and am familiar with but by no means the only ones available on the market. I am not invested in any of these companies but recommend their services.

BOOKS

Hydraulic Die Forming for Jewelers & Metalsmiths by Susan Kingsley
Patina: 300+ Coloration Effects for Jewelers & Metalsmiths by Matthew Runfola

METAL SUPPLIERS

Rio Grande, riogrande.com
Metalliferous, metalliferous.com
Rings and Things, rings-things.com

DIES AND HYDRAULIC PRESSES

Potter USA, potterusa.com
Rio Grande, riogrande.com
Harbor Freight Tools, harborfreight.com

ACRYLIC SHEET

Lowe's, lowes.com
Home Depot, homedepot.com

PRISMACOLOR PREMIER COLORED PENCILS

Michaels, michaels.com
A. C. Moore, acmoore.com

PATINA

Jax, jaxchemical.com
Novacan, novacan.net
Sculpt Nouveau, sculptnouveau.com

SEALER

ProtectaClear by Everbrite, everbritecoating.com

PROJECT INDEX

Flower Pendant
25

Heart of My Heart Pendant
37

Waves of Blue Pendant
43

Geometric Design Pendant
47

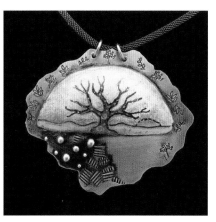

Tree of Life Pendant
51

Fourth of July Pendant
55

Blooming Flowers Bracelet
59

Green Jewel of the Nile Pendant
69

Celestial Spiral Pendant
75